Getting on with the World

poems by

Lynn Veach Sadler

Finishing Line Press
Georgetown, Kentucky

Getting on with the World

Copyright © 2017 by Lynn Veach Sadler
ISBN 978-1-63534-127-0 First Edition
All rights reserved under International and Pan-American Copyright Conventions.
No part of this book may be reproduced in any manner whatsoever without written
permission from the publisher, except in the case of brief quotations embodied in critical
articles and reviews.

Publisher: Leah Maines

Editor: Christen Kincaid

Cover Art: pixabay.com/en/flower-bright-white-art-iris-1425294/

Author Photo: Ms. A. J. Hallett

Cover Design: Elizabeth Maines

Printed in the USA on acid-free paper.
Order online: www.finishinglinepress.com
         also available on amazon.com

               Author inquiries and mail orders:
                   Finishing Line Press
                     P. O. Box 1626
               Georgetown, Kentucky 40324
                       U. S. A.

Table of Contents

Not in the Holy Month of Ramadan 1

Not Race But Culture 3

The Grey Wolf Comes again 4

The *Irish* Travelers (Or Is It *World?*) 6

Ava Gardner "Shades" the Grave of Gregory Peck 7

Lt. Col. Ely Parker Tells His Daughter of Grant and Lee 9

What If . . . ? 11

Purple Irises 13

The Making of Days 15

Milk 16

The Egg Came Live again 18

Back Story for Kerouac 20

Getting on with the World 21

After You're Dead 23

Blasé New York City after "Once Upon a Time" 24

Stoning(s) 25

By the Pricking of Einstein's Thumbs 26

Disinformation 27

If Annie Leibovitz Did a "Hanukkah Retrospective" 28

Teenager 29

Levitation 30

Not in the Holy Month of Ramadan

The history of Oman
floods with wars over water—
but not on our day in Muscat
when it rains camels for
the only non-monsoon time in twenty-one years.

Sultan Said is a Bahla magician of progress,
but his prescience has fallen short of drains.
For days, the rains have kept the dhows in port.
Cars stall; men daintily lift their *dishdashas*.
Will floods flow
from the sharp, dark mountains?
Children dig in the moistened earth;
teenaged boys dance, wave at our passing bus.
Might the women leave *abayas* in abeyance,
drop their black masks?
Mutrah Suk is flooded,
its shops mostly closed.
We wait in the rain for our bus.
An Omani in lavender *dishdasha*, pleated turban,
invites me for coffee, tea—or more?
He wears no rhinoceros-horn-handled *khanjar*,
but that symbol of virility lurks somewhere.

Later, I return to the suk via ship's shuttle.
With others, I enter by an alleyway upstream.
The lane between the shops is two feet wide,
of stone, once-packed earth, some tile,
running water, caroming umbrellas.
Sans the souvenir stands, the shops are elegant.
Aglow in rainy dark, they cascade gold, silver,
caftans, Kashmir shawls, colorwheels of cloth.
Tourists take tolas of silver, jeweled oryxes.
Much of the gold jewelry is bridal wear.
(But only the groom attends both receptions.)

No mention of myrrh,
but frankincense abounds.
Prayers ride to Heaven
on frankincense fumes;
women perfume their hair in its smoke.

In the Arab world, to stare is not rude.
Today, in the rainy twilight
of the male world

1

of Muscat's Mutrah Suk,
in the land of imams and sultans,
in warm rain
like rose or orange-blossom water,
the eye contact is more than obligatory.
This is not the Holy Month of Ramadan,
and I
am a
Western woman
alone.

Not Race But Culture

"Evolution" still raises hackles,
but Darwin was cautious with the term.
After all, he knew barnacles
(and differences among barnacle geese!).

He also might have coined,
but cautiously didn't,
"not race but culture."
John Edmonstone, freed slave,

rather similar, I think, to
the effect of Equiano on Wilberforce,
didn't just teach him taxidermy
but life in the rainforest,

whereupon, divagating later,
Darwin-fashion (body and mind),
Darwin concluded that,
superficial differences

in appearance notwithstanding,
"Negroes and Europeans" are
well and truly related.
Were this view bruited about

even today, brouhaha would
burden the scientific bunch,
though, so far as I am aware,
Darwin was mistaken only about finches.

The Grey Wolf Comes again

Kara's Turkish grandfather lived with her family,
taught her the language, recited poetry,
explained how poetry always spoke for the nation.
He gave her the oral poetry of feats of the *Akritai*,
lords of the borders between Byzantine and Arab lands;
ceded her the *Book of Dede Korkut*, Turkish national epic.

Kara feels compelled to serve Turkish poetry.
Her followers' password
is a Turkish proverb from the poet Baki:
"What endures in this dome is but a pleasant sound."
She's learned to dervish an apple dance
to *saz* or lute and *nây*, reed flute,
chanting their *zikr* or dirge.
Ziya Gökalp's collected poems
are *Kizil Elma, The Red Apple*.
The Red Apple Tree is the Turkish Paradise,
the great city to which their destiny leads them.

The *pièce de résistance* is
the legend of the Grey Wolf
leading the Turks from the steppes
of Central Asia to their homeland.
The first to embody it was Mustafa Kemal,
Father-Turk, in Panama hat,
head gear always making
a political statement in Turkey—
turban to fez, which Atatürk condemned.
Now this Turkish-talking
American woman appears
in grey-fur-lined white hood
(purchased by her grandfather).
And Kara's own poem
has gone out among the people:

>Rome on seven hills.
>We are Golden-Horned
>Byzantium, Constantinople, Istanbul.

>We are *Nova Roma*
>built on seven hills,
>knowing seven ways to enlightenment.

She-Wolf suckled Romulus and Remus,
founders of Great Rome.
Mother-Goddess Kubabat led us forth.

She became the Greeks' Cybele.
Shams al-Din disappeared,
left Jalal al-Din Muhammad Rumi

to mourn in verse.
Sufi Shams al-Din has come again.
Grey Wolf led us from the steppes.

In famine and drought
throughout all Anatolia,
wolves howled in the streets of Istanbul.

Grey Wolf, our Father-Turk, came
to grow a modern state.
We need Grey Wolf again, and

she is come.
She comes like a *sufi* man of wool.
She comes in mineral white

like leavings of
the thermal springs of Pamukkale-
Hierapolis, the baths the Romans loved,

the baths for which
Paul called the Laodiceans
"neither hot nor cold."

To turn away
is to enter the cave Plutonium,
to disappear into the Underworld,

to be again Sick Man of Europe.
Turkey needs the Tanzimat—
reforms—again.

"When they're ready for me," Kara says,
"I'll come in, go underground.
Things are improving. Earlier,
Nazim Hikmet, a 'subversive' poet,
had to write in prison."

The *Irish* Travelers (Or Is It *World*?)

The "Gypsies" of my childhood probably
descended from those nomadic
"Irish Travelers" or Pavees (called by some
"puretee Jews" and linked with the tinsmith
cursed for building the cross
on which Jesus died.) Cromwell drove
one branch from Ireland.

I never connected "tinkers" with Gypsies,
now wonder if my grandfather,
who traveled selling Watkins products,
was an Irish Traveler Gypsy, though some sources
deny their being Gypsies
(considered Asian Indian) and relate them to
pre-Celts (the Fairy Queen Mab) and Celts
far older than the likes of King Arthur.
Many still wander; speak among themselves
the ancient "Cant" or "Gammon";
maintain clannish ways—
"looping" (a mating ritual),
marrying young, valuing males.
They have such settlements as
Murphy Village in South Carolina,
stand accused of being scam artists,
are caught in a time warp of our
and their own stereotyping,
remain a Resident Boogie Man.
Even Madonna's championing
has recently brought jeers.

Why can't we distinguish figures
"allowed" in childhood legendry
from the flesh-and-blood HUMANS
who walk through our adult worlds daily,
suffering from such labels as
"Irish Traveler," "Gypsy"?
Will we accept the DNA that validates
tow-headed Romas?
Who's next?

Ava Gardner "Shades" the Grave of Gregory Peck

We were the King and Queen of Beauty,
you and I. Maybe that's why we could just be friends.
Still, I know you were too good for me, Old Friend.
I have had no good from men except your friendship.
Women *and* men liked *you*.

Your earliest childhood was mean and lonely.
Mine was lean and hungry—but crowded.
I never had a child. Your son committed suicide.
You would have said it was better to have loved
and lost than be childless.

I *copied* literature—*movies*, I should say—
expatriated myself to slinky Spain à la Brett Ashley,
but I was no lady like the Lady Brett.
You? Before Atticus Finch was, you were.
Lewt McCanles? *Not ever!* You were the all-time
Poster Boy for Good Guys, and you a native Californian!

You never thought I was
what my tobacco-barning kin
call a "slut." You knew I had to *play* one.
I know it was no cinch to be Finch,
placed as you were. I was placed where you were.
I *know*. You managed your Hemingway
without all the masculine stuff
humming like a humming bird in heat.
You were . . . *solid*.

You told me I was too hard on myself
and other people. When biographers seized on
my wedding "Mickey Rooney
shortly after joining Metro,"
you said, "Count the '*shortly*'
as magnificent pun, not puny obsession."
That's the way you dealt with all the hype
of your being such an "*acti*vist," you said.

Not just Broadway, but *The Stage* loved *you*.
That time you were filming in my home state,
took the flowers to my grave,
you told those state Supreme Court justices
how their daughters should go
if acting careers were what they wanted.
You set out the true *Peck*ing order:

local theater, then Broadway, then Hollywood.
Did you really do "thirty-some plays
in community theater"?
I know about your helping found
the La Jolla Playhouse.

You got away with being a Democrat!
A "liberal"!
What if you *had* challenged Governor Ronnie?
You *lived* all the causes you fought for.
You were pro-Blacks, anti-Semitism,
made another stand with *Pork Chop Hill*
(which is *still relevan*t, I'd say).
Me? Liberal the wrong way, I suppose.
But I'm proud I was friend to Lena Horne,
though she didn't eulogize at my funeral
the way Brock Peters did at yours.
Well, I didn't march with Mr. King,
postpone the Oscars when he was assassinated.
Of all your awards, the Medal of Freedom
suits you best in my opinion.

As we speak, my home state's
having another flap about a book.
The Quran was last year.
This time "they're" "nickeling and diming"
Ms. "Erringright," as you would doubtless deem her.
Does she—anybody—know you helped Chrysler save
its six hundred thousand jobs?

You were too good for me, Old Friend.
When I came here—*died* seems too incisive for *me*—
you took in my Carmen and Morgan.
My leavings: a loyal housekeeper,
a dog as loyal as dogs can be.
You had a "real boy's dog," you told me.
I should have named mine "Gregory."
No, "Eldred," Old Friend.
"Eldred" sounds as Welsh as my Welsh Corgi . . . .
Surely, "Emlyn" is Welch. Emlyn Williams'
The Morning Star—your debut on Broadway.
You've been *morning, noon* . . .
now *evening* STAR, Old Friend. You were
"The Man for All Seasons." *No act.*
You were too good for me, Old Friend.
That was *no act* either.

Lt. Col. Ely Parker Tells His Daughter of Grant and Lee

The ninth day of April.
The year of the White Man's Lord 1865.
Appomattox Court House.
The Wilmer McLean home.

I transcribed ("beautiful cursive")
six copies of the Confederate Terms of Surrender.
(Had drafted two of the articles
for Gen. Grant's approval.)
Once both sides had agreed
upon the conditions,
I copied them in a manifold book.

Grant, trying to put Lee at ease, I suppose,
discussed the Mexican War.
In the midst of ending a terrible war—
one Ulysses afterwards,
not that day,
kept referring to as
"the rebellion"—
they talked of another war.
(They claim we Indians
are the warlike people!)
Gen. Grant could not stop
talking about the past.
Finally, Gen. Lee
had to remind him,
politely, gently,
why they were meeting.

Gen. Grant introduced each of us,
his staff, to Gen. Lee,
who shook our hands.
When he reached me,
there was a pause,
a reaction of a kind.

Some said he was affronted,
believing Gen. Grant to have forced
a person of color upon him.
We Indians,

as you know well, my Maudie,
are still called,
with the Black Man's race, "colored."

I do not think such was the case with Lee.
No, I believe Gen. Lee recognized
the momentousness of the moment,
aside from its relation to the dying war.
His pause was brief,
and then he said,
"I am glad to see
one real American here."

I thought even then of the honor
he did my Red people.
I expect History
to seize upon it yet.

I answered him carefully,
hoping he would
understand my honor to
his Southern people—
"We are *all* Americans."
I meant it for a curative,
hoped (did not expect it to)
History would seize upon it.

What If . . . ?

I, José de San Martín,
had to ask your help.
I was beholden.
You were subtle, but you . . .
pressed the case.
Had you not been subtle . . . .

We both turned on Spain,
wanted our countries free of Spanish yoke.
You in the north.
I freed the south lands . . .
Argentina, Chile. If only I had not had to
have your aid in Peru.
If only . . . .

I was beholden.
Can you feel how I felt
when you became dictator of Peru?
(You had been—yes, but a short time—
dictator of Venezuela.)
I refused Chilean presidency
in favor of my Chilean lieutenant, General O'Higgins.
Oh, I know you would point out
your thrusting forward Francisco de Miranda.
You saw, found distasteful
the coronation of Napoleon.
You wrote so much.
The "Cartagena Manifesto" . . .
the "Jamaica Letter" . . . .
That unfortunate loss of your wife
to fever . . . . Such a noble figure you cut!
Though a wealthy aristocrat,
you spoke for us colonials.
You claimed to know
the "character Spanish American."

Your mighty certainty of
"what the 'Spanish American'
is not yet ready for"!
We colonials had not
dined on, with you,
the "Age of Enlightenment."
You could not trust us as "federalists."

I know, I know.

I was for a monarchy.
But the *president* you proposed was,
in all but name, a monarch.
You wanted
a confederation of South American states.
You wanted
the British parliamentary way,
yet claimed to know our character.

Oh, I crossed the Alps, too!
(Figuratively—at our Guayaquil Conference, 1822.
It was no "conference"!)

But I was beholden to you, Simón Bolívar . . . .
I left my country quietly.
But you did not, finally,
get your way.
What if . . . ?

Purple Irises

Our gray guide is *still* incredulous.
"They shelled Dubrovnik!
Dubrovniks have no fights with nobody.
Croats and Serbs always lived here together."

Did he go gray when the war came down?
Shells from the hills and mountains?
Which grayed first?
His hair? Mustache?
His skin? His clothes?

I am incredulous, too.
I see purple irises growing wild.
"Who transplanted them?" I think.
"Who divided the bulbs?"

The guide talks on,
musing to himself.
"They shell from mountains.
They killing mostly children and young.
Why would they shell Dubrovnik?
It is UNESCO World Heritage Site.
The world become angry with them.
How do you say it?
They shoot themselves in foot.
The world took up our case."

It is spring's eve.
Lavender, Scottish Broom,
tiny yellow flowers just beginning to re-bloom.
I look for more irises growing wild.
Every clod of space in hilly, boulderous yards
gives itself to grapes' brown roots,
vegetables, potatoes mostly,
no space for flowers.

The soil, rich and brown,
has been brought in,
tilled and turned.

"Such a shame," the guide is saying.
"The Communists taught us not to be self-reliant."

"Emerson," I think.

"Emerson and purple irises."

"Our youth will not plow and plant our earth.
We could have agriculture
as our pride, our mainstay.
We would not have to plead
with tourists to return.
But our youth flock to cities,
claim they cannot find the jobs,
will not take the jobs finding them.
The government is about to stop
paying them to be unemployed.
What will they do then? What will Dubrovnik do?"

I re-write Whitman.
"'When *irises* last in the courtyard bloomed.'
Do irises spoil prosody?" I ponder.

Our gray guide moroses on.
"I think, no matter what they claim,
Montenegro wanted us Dubrovniks.
Dubrovnik is the whole of Croatia's crown jewel.
Here is where the tourists come.
We would be good taking."

I imagine I see an iris
breaking gray, granitic ground.
Something like a crocus.
The hills are alive with the sound of . . .
irises pushing out.

We reach the fork,
turn left away from Montenegro.

"We let in few
across Montenegro's border now.
They crossed to our side
pretending to be tourists like you.
Then they take out guns, shoot us down."

I wish he'd commented on the irises.
Their tuberous roots.
Their green-sword leaves.
Their flowers—small in Dubrovnik
but all purple.

The Making of Days

At the local buffet joint after I recited my poem
honoring those from my home county
dead in Nam—
three aging hippies.
Refugees not just from Nam.
Bandannas, torn t-shirts.
Sweaty, dirty. Paunched,
despite the motorcycles
they've parked in front of
the restaurant's window.

They keep looking my way,
ignore my husband.
"Aren't you the one . . . ?"
He's loud enough
to pull the restaurant's attention.
I nod. Over they come.
I stand to meet them.
They pause. The leader
clears his throat. "I never thought I'd hear
the sort of things you said."
"Much less from a female,"
I think, don't voice.
They stick out their hands.
I don't shake but hug them.
They nod, walk away,
tears in all eyes, mine included.

I wish Clint Eastwood had been there,
with the threesome from *Easy Rider*.
It would have made their day, too.

But later I thought—
they would have accepted *Peter* Fonda,
but can *Jane* ever go home again?
But, then, do the current Wall Street protesters
even know about Abbie Hoffman throwing dollars
onto the floor of the New York Stock Exchange?

Milk

A breast pump!
It's embarrassing. And it hurts!
Eight days, and I'll dry up.
God made the whole world in six.
We've made war somewhere
in the whole world in five,
milked the world (before it milks us?).

Eight days, and Operation Desert-Storm
will be over, dried up, and a lot of our troops
will come home to dry *out*.
As in every war in every place
all over the world.

Eight days . . . . I've got to dry up *now*,
before somebody hears me groaning,
sees me holding myself,
my breasts, this way.
I must get a *hold* on myself. Get a *grip*!
Or an Iraqi SCUD missile
will dry me up permanently.
Think—milk of . . . milk of human kindness!

The baby—I knew the call could come any time.
I can't expect the Army to do call-ups
at my convenience. Get a life!
Get an *Army* life!
Or just settle for the one it's given me.
Nursing! *Nurse*! I'm an Army *nurse*.
An officer in the Army Nurse Corps.
Act like it! The baby—
The baby won't even know I'm gone.
She's a baby. What do babies know?
Now if it were a teenager, say,
or a middle schooler even . . . .

. . .

I survived the first one, didn't I?
I'll survive Operation Iraqi Freedom.
I *will*. It's just . . . this party hat, birthday horn,
celebration for Mindy. I never learn, do I?
My sister can take Mindy to Chuck E. Cheese's,
handle the birthday party.

I knew the notice could come any time.

I can't expect the Army to do call-ups
at my kid's convenience. *My* convenience.
Get a life! Get an *Army* life!
My famous refrain: "What do babies know . . . ?"
Well, she's going on thirteen now. She knows.
She knows war, what it does to her family.

Somebody has to protect the world, sure,
but not *me*, not *me*.
Yes, *me*. Milk of human kindness.
Stop it! Cool it! I'm in. I've *been* in.
I just have to hang on a bit longer to retire.

Tell Mindy how biblical this area is,
the magic here. "The Tigris and Euphrates Rivers.
The ruins of Babylon,
its Hanging Gardens one of the Seven Wonders
of the Ancient World.
A miracle in the middle of the desert.
Exotic plants and animals.
All holy sites have been declared
'no-target zones,' Mindy.
Najaf is here—third holiest Arab city
after Mecca and Medina,
and they're in Saudi Arabia.
Read up on it all, Mindy.

You need to know about
all God's world, other cultures.
And remember, Mindy, we talked about
Abraham being from Ur—it's in southern Iraq."
(Have we already *Ur*red too much?)

Mindy watches re-reruns of *China Beach*.
Put *them* macho nurses in your Abrams tank
before they roll right over you!

I, Dorothy-Nursie, am not in
Operation Desert-Storm any longer.
I, Dorothy-Nursie, am in
Operation Iraqi Freedom.
My wars runneth over like my milk of yesteryear.
(Have I been milked?)

If my milk is spilled, let it be as
the milk of human kindness.

The Egg Came Live again

I was old, had learned.
I felt feathered Cape of the Condor
stir in its icy cave on Mount Aconcagua
when The-Miss-Addie came among us.
She was young but destined.

I took her to the Patron's secret cellar
where his Condor Room trophies were prepared.
He called himself El Caudillo, The Condor.
The smell—not to be masked by all
the orange petals of Buenos Aires' *elegantes*.

Odor of the Saladero,
slaughtering grounds at city's edge.
The cages permitted not their wingspread.
"*Nunca más!*" The-Miss-Addie cried,
kicking rack of blood-tipped taunting spears.

She unlatched the cage of She-Condor,
who waited until her mate was free
before stepping out. Then the great condors
sang together one holding triumphant note.
Iron grillwork melted from windows.

The condors flew for our sacred Andes cave.
The-Miss-Addie, in white flowing dress,
stood upon back of He-Condor,
laughing in the stream of cold, clean air.
In the cave, down stepped Our-Miss-Addie,

dressed in Cape of Condor.
The condors used their beaks
to pull its great head onto hers.
Wild El Caudillo came then,
mist drawing back from him.

When he lunged for Our-Miss-Addie,
she stepped away as if from
bull unworthy. El Caudillo, stunned,
opened his huge mouth, roared.
Serpents curled from out its corners.
He could not re-close his mouth.
The Good Three watched,
serpents piling about them.

When time was, He-Condor lifted talon,
placed it on the ring of serpents.

Serpents disappeared. El Caudillo stood,
mouth frozen in skull's grin.
The condors took him from the cave,
head in her beak, one leg in his.
The-Miss-Addie stepped out onto

the condors' nesting ledge,
looked in the sacred nest,
took off her Condor Cape,
placed it over the egg.
The egg came live again.

Back Story for Kerouac

Jack Kerouac's friend, the Black cook
Old Glory, died on the *Dorchester*
that day. Jack could have, too.

Kerouac deemed his "dead brother"
a saint, heard him speak from Heaven.
Jack, a scat-singing cat,

jazz-Massed Gregorian chants,
left the Navy for "angel tendencies,"
roamed the earth.

Getting on with the World

We were docked in Aqaba, Jordan.
I stopped by the ship's Java Bar.
As I lapped my latté,
I heard the woman say—
from her preamble,
she lives in Florida
but was born in Israel,
mostly travels the world,
has seen a thing or two—
her hand punctuating
with the "eh" sign all the way,

"An Arab is an Arab is an Arab.
A little desert man.
They let him out with oil.
And now because of oil,
he sits among the leaders of the world
making decisions for the world.
Well, he can't make decisions for Israel.
Keep him in the desert.
He's a Bedouin.
A little desert man.
One of these days,
Israel will get tired of it all again
and bomb the shit out of
those little desert men,
say to the world,
'World, what do you think of that?'
I'm not religious, but
I know the Bible for its history.
The Bible says, 'Trouble will come
out of the North.'
It means the little desert men.
They took what they wanted
from the Old Testament.
Yes, their language is Semitic.

But Jews and Arabs never will be friends!
Their cultures are different.
You can't change a person's culture.
We have to accept that
Jews and Arabs never will be friends
and get on with the world.
America says it won the war with
the desert man Sadam.

Bush counted all the way,
proclaimed the Hundred Days' War,
said he'd won.
Hell, all he did was bomb.
And mostly his bombs went wrong.
Sadam and his high-and-mighty
brought in piles of little desert men,
little desert farmers,
stacked them in the trenches.
Sadam and his high-and-mighty
burrowed deep as Hell.
They had their gas, but that was all.
Their gas and oil.
He would have bombed Israel,
but all he had was gas.
When he attached it to the bombs,
they were too heavy,
couldn't reach to Israel.
I won't watch goddamn CNN!
All it does on Israel is the Gaza Strip
and Golan Heights!
There're hot spots all over the world.
In goddamn America, more people are
killed in a day by robbers and murderers
than in a year in Israel.
The whole world's going to be run
by murderers and thugs.
The little desert men buy them with oil.

Only fools watch goddamn CNN!
Now Colin Powell plans to provoke
to finish the job Old Bush started
for New Bush—
but mainly for Colin Powell.
We need a Burning Bush,
but New Bush can 'Burn, Bush, Burn!'
He'll be a burning Bush at most.
Any Burning Bush will
come from Israel."

Suddenly I knew
why she was familiar.
Last night's performer!
She'd ended her stage show
with "Let There Be Peace on Earth"
("... and let it begin with me.").

After You're Dead

Plato said poets lied.
Poets used to use "personas."
See especially John Donne.
How many now would get
"personas," much less "personae"?
If I as poet write an excuse for Bin Laden—

I have. A ballad about his loving
a "Jewish maid." All four parents
more-than-object. During the raid
after her Bin Laden leads,
her father stabs her to keep her from "that Arab."
Bin Laden declares jihad.

If I as poet write an excuse for Bin Laden,
would it be published?
If so, would jihad be declared against me?
Would Jews and Arabs frown?
Would the world look askance,
pronounce me mad?

Freedom of speech in poetry?
Only that in your journal
for after you're dead.

Blasé New York City after "Once Upon a Time"

Post-September 11, 2001,
the Soup Nazi changed his name
to "Soup Nicely" and not only feeds the poor
but smiles at them, serving up on the side
"Peace Pâté upon The Bread of Life."

Post-September 11, 2001,
we lowered the crime rate
by applying a technique of Ancient Turkey
to what was left of New York
and solving much of our racial friction.
We shifted the races around.
Put Dutch, Filipinos, and Indonesians here,
we said; they're simpatico.
If Blacks and Jews won't mix,
try the former with Yemenites.
Throw Italians and Russians together.
We started the Mafia-to-*Mafiya* transfer.
(So the Genoveses roared again
and moved to Jersey.
Brighton Beach straightened right up
into card-carrying hard-liners.
Fire Island was left to itself.)
Nobody was dissed, just displaced.
Citizens were given incentives, including
centers to teach interpersonal skills
and English and jobs beyond
"swimming the Yellow River" [driving a taxi].
If citizens wanted to live in a "Hybrid Community,"
that was arranged. We made no hash
of the Melting Pot. Our success rate was 93.2%!

You woke up today believing New York's
strangest intersection the corner of
Waverly Place and Waverly Place.
Wrong! Not post-September 11, 2001.

Stoning(s)

Ripe for stoning. May and December
on a voyage round the world. How the women hate her.
How the men gawk. He's a hundred-and-four,
in wheelchair. She's a fit-and-feisty forty.
"Well, it wasn't for her looks or dress code!"
She prefers short leather, midriff bare, jewelry big
in places kinky, a pointed witch's hat, but brown
in the few patches barren of souvenir pins.
"I heard she was a harlot!" "I heard she was his nurse!"
"His sons are dead long-since.
His grandson is suing her. He's coming on in Singapore
to get Grandpops off the ship
before she wrests all their Jewish wealth from him.
She lives in the shops spending all she can
before the litigation ties her snatching hands."
"Every morning before five, she's at the front desk,
going through her deposit boxes, jewelry spread
out on the counter, cigarette hanging from
both corners of her mouth, drinking a magnum of
champagne straight from the bottle."
"Do you think they're really married?"
"The stewards won't go to their penthouse alone
because she lies around nude, yells for them to enter."
"The Captain had to have a talk,
place the public lounges off limits."
"That was after she came on to him."
"She's not allowed to drink now, except in her suite."
 "I don't want to be on the same tour bus.
I hear she's on the scenic river cruise tomorrow.
Maybe she'll fall overboard and drown!"

Hey, why don't you pray for that very thing!
So much easier than stoning, if not nearly so much fun.
How'd you like *The Stoning of Soraya M.*?
How do you feel about the impending
Sakineh Mohammadi Ashtiani stoning?
Is stoning just niqabs and burqas to you?

By the Pricking of Einstein's Thumbs

Everyone knows Einstein of $E = MC^2$.
But do you know the Einstein
who discovered the principle of relativity
by imagining himself traveling on a beam of light?
The Einstein who could not base this conviction
on logical reasons?
The Einstein whose only witness was
the pricking of his little finger?
(Shakespeare predicted the Anti-Matter Einstein
in *Macbeth's* Second Witch,
and I, by my poetic license, claim *title* to him.)
Do you know the Einstein convinced
that the world could be described
only in terms of "mental probabilities"?
The Einstein who thought the Mysterious
the most beautiful experience humans can have?
The Einstein who deemed the Mysterious
the fundamental emotion standing at the cradle
of true art and true science?
Who felt that, whoever does not know the Mysterious
and can no longer wonder, no longer marvel,
is as good as dead, and his eyes are dimmed?
The Einstein who found his most difficult thinking
enjoyable and like a daydream?
The Einstein who declared that overemphasis
on the competitive system and premature specialization
on the ground of immediate usefulness
kill the spirit on which all cultural life depends,
specialized knowledge included?
Do you know the Einstein who knew
what the individual can do?
Einstein's individual can give a fine example
and have the courage to uphold—firmly—
ethical convictions in a society of cynics.

Disinformation

So much disinformation about us.
Not by our choice. *This* Navajo code talk is
not for the ears of the enemy,
but for the ears of Americans, all races.
We didn't start in World War II.
We worked in World War I,
Korea, early on in Nam.
We weren't just Marines.
We weren't just Native Americans.
We code talkers were Basques.
The British used Welsh native speakers.
(Was any Yiddish used?)
We weren't just American.
The Cherokees were, albeit momentarily,
under British command.
We weren't alone, we Navajos.
We code talkers were Cherokees, Choctaws,
Comanches, Iowan Meskwaki . . . .
Many predated Navajos in the code-talk game.
Navajo code talkers weren't just Navajo.
Philip Johnston, son of a missionary to us,
proposed us to the Marines
(who still use some of our code terms).
We Indians aren't entirely solemn-serious.
We can be sly-funny.
We wish we'd thought of
the Comanches' "crazy white man" for Hitler.
We weren't just code talkers.
What we mainly were,
all of us code talkers, was CODE CRACKERS.
We cracked—exploded—
the code that said Indians and Blacks
were cannon fodder, slackers;
that "tribes" couldn't
work together, have commonalities,
work side by side with Whites.
The main code we cracked was STEREOTYPES.

If Annie Leibovitz Did a "Hanukkah Retrospective"

If Annie Leibovitz did a "Hanukkah Retrospective,"
throughout it all, rolling stones,
candles burning at both ends

with Millay in her accustomed restlessness.
Eight candles flame (fumé),
not successively,

in hair of AllGoddesses.
Woman presses olives
in her red boxing gloves.

Yoko and a female golem hug.
Yoko (not her Samurai face) naked,
John clothed.

Bathsheba (or is it Salome?) a-dance
among the pillars of
King Solomon's Temple.

A Muslim woman and a showgirl
hora together,
Leibovitz reaching in to flick the burka.

Osceola McCarty passes out gelt,
washing each piece first,
in her day dress, not her wig and red suit.

A(n) half-hour away,
Eudora rises from her blue chair
to step upon the porch,

"But why would you want *my* picture?"
Miners, showgirls, other power women,
Lucinda Williams singing as she writes . . . .

Aging hanging in the air
like light particles
from imaginary Hanukkahs Past.

Miracle of women's oil on troubled *others*.
Not just for Hanukkah,
My Honey-from-the-Lioness!

Teenager

I think people are like the loggerhead
(in more ways than one!) turtles.
Loggerheads have these
magnetic fields to navigate by.
They don't *have* to use them.
They can leave their "gyre" and die
from the frigid waters outside it.
The fact remains, they have these
magnetic markers, these genetic imprints,
to find their way by.
I wish I could find mine.
[What *did* Yeats mean by
"turning and turning in the widening gyre"?
Then there's Lewis Carroll's Jabberwocky's
"Did gyre and gimble in the wabe" (?).]

I read that Iggy Pop
gets some of his weirdness
from jazz. He claims he heard
the jazz sax "float," so he tried to.
My favorite song in the world,
from a musical at least, is
"The Last Night of the World,"
from *Miss Saigon*, especially the part about
"A song/Played on a solo saxophone/
A crazy sound/A lonely sound."
I wish the saxophone were my instrument.
I wish its "lonely sound" didn't aim at me.

Ms. Ellerby, my English teacher,
told us about the old sport
of swinging cats by their tails
as targets for archers.
That's how I feel a lot of the time.
Like the cat, not the archer.

Levitation

Former center of the Boston Celtics Bill Russell
knew when the basketball game went magical,
when play rose to a new level:
both teams were at peak performance;
the referees were flying, too.
That mystical feeling came
when three or four of those on the floor
would *levitate*, become catalysts for the others.
At that special level, the game would be
in the white heat of competition,
but Russell would not feel competitive.
He could sense—see—how the next play would develop
and where the next shot would be taken.
The spells were fragile, did not last.
Bill Russell is talking wholeness, learning,
the chill/quiver/goose bumps
running up and down the nape of your neck
when you are the teacher in the classroom
(or the person wherever) and everything is just right;
you can do no wrong for a small magical while,
and you know it. Bill Russell is talking
physical, mental, and magical;
conscious but mostly subconscious;
odd things but mostly the sensing of odd things;
the fact that sports (or whatever we do) can be art;
learning as collaboration with oneself and with others;
the white heat of competition but no competition;
each person higher and better
and the whole higher and better still;
what students *should* have and *should* witness in the classroom;
the *creative tension* between
being an individual and being part of a team;
Deming's "continuous improvement";
Peter Senge's "personal mastery"
and "living in a continual learning mode";
Stephen Covey's "private victory";
Keats's "Negative Capability";
Coleridge's "willing suspension of disbelief";
the ability of the Metaphysical poets to combine disparates;
oxymoron and paradox; the whole human dance,
that precarious perch at the top of Jacob's ladder,
with one foot in heaven and one below,
and the dream that lets you see *if you will*
and choose *if you will*.

Getting on with the World: **Acknowledgments**

"Not in the Holy Month of Ramadan." Winner, 1998 Howl Awards, *The Lone Wolf Review*, 2.1 (1998): 1. Third Place, Arizona State Poetry Society, Thirtieth Annual Contest, 1997. *Sandcutters: Journal of the Arizona State Poetry Society* (Winter, 1997/98): 43. Highly Commended Award, Tom Howard Poetry Contest, 2006. *Sailing in the Mist of Time.* In press.

"Not Race But Culture." Winner, National Writer's Contest, 2009, *City Works Journal*, San Diego City College, 16 (2009): 2, 8. *The Taylor Trust*, 2 (April-June, 2009): 32.

"The Grey Wolf Comes again." *Slant*, 17 (Summer 2003): 78-80.

"The *Irish* Travelers. (Or Is It *World*?)." *2016 Voices Israel Anthology*. In press.

"Ava Gardner 'Shades' the Grave of Gregory Peck." *The Copperfield Review* [on-line], 6.5 (Spring, 2006). *Sensations Magazine,* Cinema Issue, 34 (Summer 2004): 24. *Ava Gardner: Touches of Venus.* Gilbert L. Gigliotti, Ed. (Washington, D. C.: Entasis Press, 2010): 142-144.

"Lt. Col. Ely Parker Tells His Daughter of Grant and Lee." *Golden Poetry: A Celebration of Southern Poets 50 and Older, Poetry of the Golden Generation, II.* Kennesaw State University: Kennesaw, GA. Brumby Holdings, Inc.: A Legacies Book Publication, 2004. 106-108. Honorable Mention, Newburyport Art Association [Newburyport, MA], 2004.

"What If . . . ?" As "San Martín Thinks Upon the Secret Guayaquil Conference, 1822," *HIMS.* Ed. elizaBeth Benson-Udom. Danville, CA: elizaPress Publications, 2007 Eclectic Anthology Series, #4: 212-213.

"Purple Irises." First Place, Fifth National Poetry Contest, Northwest Ohio Branch, National League of American Pen Women, 2001. Semi-finalist, 2001 Emily Dickinson Poetry Award, Universities West Press. *The 2001 Emily Dickinson Award Anthology. A Commemorative Edition of the Best Poems of 2001.* Flagstaff, AZ: Universities West Press, 2002: 58-60. *Lynn Veach Sadler: Greatest Hits, 1995-2001.* Pudding House's (Invitational) National Archiving Project, Poets' Greatest Hits. Johnstown, Ohio: Pudding House Publications, 2002: 33. *the new renaissance,* 12.2 (2005): 77-79. Most Highly Recommended Award, Tom Howard Poetry Contest, 2010.

"The Making of Days." From "Voices on Vietnam." Lynn Veach Sadler, *Brother, Can You Spare a War?* Grimbergen, Belgium: Aquillrelle Press, 2011: 182-185.

"Milk." *Working Title: Selections from the Second Annual Skysaje Poetry Contest.* Rochester, NY: CFK Publications, 2006: 16-18. Selected for "A

Family Is . . . ," 2006 Exhibition, Northwest Cultural Council.

"The World Egg Came Live Again." Lynn Veach Sadler, *Brother, Can You Spare a War?* Grimbergen, Belgium: Aquillrelle Press, 2011: 134-135.

"Back Story for Kerouac," *Voices Israel 2011*, 37 (2011): 149. As "Jazz Mass for Kerouac's Navy," *Between the Lines: A Book of Words, Poetry Festival Chapbook, 2010*. Wilmington: Art Soup, 2010. Unnumbered.

"Getting on with the World." *Mining* [Chapbook]. Greensboro, NC: March Street Press, 2009: 2-4.

"After You're Dead." Second Place, *Scratch* Winter Quarterly Contest. On the *Scratch* website. *Scratch* 2011 print anthology, in press. *A Bird in the Hand—Risk and Flight*. Ed. Whitney Scott. Crete, Illinois: Outrider Press, 2011. In press. *Binnacle*. In press.

"Blasé New York City after 'Once Upon a Time.'" *America* [Chapbook]. Honorable Mention, 2006 Poets Corner Press Competition. Stockton, CA: Poets Corner Press, 2006: 21-22.

"Stoning(s)." Lynn Veach Sadler. *Brother, Can You Spare a War?* Grimbergen, Belgium: Aquillrelle Press, 2011: 66-67.

"By the Pricking of Einstein's Thumbs." *The Wolf Head Quarterly*, 4.2 (Spring, 1998): 36. *2001: A Science Fiction Poetry Anthology*. Ed. Keith Allen Daniels. San Francisco, CA: Anamnesis Press, 2001: 177.

"Disinformation." *Atlantic Pacific Press*, 3.4 (Winter 2010): 22-23. *Sensations Magazine: Twentieth Century America*, 47 (Spring/Summer 2010): 31. The Six Centuries Club, Rediscovering America, Poetry Research Series, New Jersey.

"If Annie Leibovitz Did a 'Hanukkah Retrospective.'" *City Works*, 12 (2005): 92-93. Honorable Mention, Annual Contest, 2005, *Poetica Magazine: Reflections of Jewish Thought* (March, 2006): 10-11.

"Teenager." Tied for first place, *Kalliope's* 2002 Sue S. Elkind Contest. *Kalliope*, 25.2 (Fall 03): 76-77. *Kalliope* cassette. First Place, 2002 National Writers Association Poetry Contest. *The Highlander II*. In press. *Left Unsaid*. In press. Middle English Literary Group. In press. *Moonwort Review*, Issue 10 (2005). Lynn Veach Sadler, *America* [Chapbook]. Honorable Mention, 2006 Poets Corner Press Competition. Stockton, CA: Poets Corner Press, 2006): 2-3.

"Levitation." *Kakalak 2009 Anthology of Carolina Poetry*. Charlotte, NC: Kakalak Poetry: 74.

A native North Carolinian and formerly a college president in Vermont, **Dr. Lynn Veach Sadler** now works full time as a creative writer and an editor. Her academic publications include 5 books and 72 articles. She has edited 22 books/proceedings and 3 national journals and writes history columns for 2 newspapers. Her first nonfiction collection is in press. As a poet, she has had 10 chapbooks and 4 full-length collections published. *Say, Brother, Can You Spare a War?* won the New England Poetry Club's 2012 Shelia Motton Award for Book of the Year. To *"Talk in That Book" of Nature* (principally Native American poems) received the (2005) Charles Dickson Chapbook Prize of the Georgia Poetry Society and was 2007 Alabama State Poetry Society Book of the Year. *Mola . . . Person* won the 2012 Evening Street Press Helen Kay Chapbook Poetry Prize. *Getting on with the World* is her 4th chapbook with Finishing Line Press. She was invited to be Visiting Scholar/Poet in Israel and judged the 2001 Voices Israel International Poetry Competition. She was published (2002) in Pudding House's (invitational) National Archiving Project, *Poets' Greatest Hits*; won *The Pittsburgh Quarterly's* 2001 Sara Henderson Hay Prize for Poetry; tied for first place in *Kalliope's* 2002 Sue S. Elkind Contest; was a runner-up for the 2002 *Spoon River Poetry Review* Editors' Prize Contest; and won the Poetry Society of America's 2003 Hemley Award and *Asphodel's* 2003 Poetry Contest. California's elizaPress named her its "2007 Writer of the Year." She won the 2009 overall award (poetry and fiction) of the San Diego City College National Writer's Contest and *City Works Journal*. As a Gilbert-Chappell Distinguished Poet 2013-2015, she mentored student and adult poets. Some 95% of her 1,300+ poems have been published.

Lynn has had 125+ short stories published and has won the North Carolina Writers' Network, *Talus and Scree, Cream City Review, Rambunctious Review, Cape Fear Crime Festival,* and *Scratch* competitions, with a number of *Glimmer Train* finalists. One story appeared in Del Sol Press's *Best of 2004: The Robert Olen Butler Prize Anthology*. Another won the Abroad Writers 2006 Competition/Fellowship (France). She has published 1 novella, 2 short story collections (another in press), and 4 novels.

In drama, Lynn has 42 plays. Her first, *Gnat* (1996), was a spin-off of the 1831 Nat

Turner uprising. *Sassing the Sphinx* was commissioned for the First International Robert Frost Symposium. *Coming Country* (Battle of New Orleans, War of 1812; libretto, lyrics) is her first musical. *Not Your Average Poet* [Frost] was a 2005 Silver Medalist in the University of Tampa's Pinter Review Prize for Drama competition. *Death Nell* won the 2005 Tampa Writers Alliance Play/Screenplay Competition; *Ms. Spam Maps of Vegas*, the Florida First Coast Writers' Festival Playwriting Contest (2007). *Second-Time-Around* (on the Iraq Wars) received Honorable Mention in the *Writer's Digest* 2006 Writing Competition and won the 2008 Judith Siegel Pearson Award at Wayne State University.

At Bennett College, Dr. Sadler set up what is thought to be the first *micro*computer laboratory in the country for teaching writing. She pioneered in Computer-Assisted Composition [CAC], coined the term, and published the first journal in the field (done with desktop publishing). From c. 1983, she consulted in and provided keynote addresses, talks, and workshops on academic computing at conferences (e.g., Association for Computers and Humanities, National Educational Computing Conference, World Conference on Computers in Education) on campuses across the U.S. and for organizations (e.g., AEtna, IBM Academic Computing Conference). She later pioneered in the adaptation of Deming and Total Quality to higher education.

Lynn has received an Extraordinary Undergraduate Teaching Award; a civil rights award from Methodist University's Black Student Movement; the Distinguished Women of NC Award for education (1992); and the Paul Jehu Barringer, Jr. and Sr., Award for Exceptional Service to the History of the State from the NC Society of Historians (2004). She was the Sanford Rotary Club's 2013 "Rotarian of the Year." She was Visiting Distinguished Scholar in the "Educational Leadership for a Competitive America" seminar of the U.S. Office of Personnel Management (1992), presented at the First International Milton Symposium (England), and directed an NEH Summer Seminar for College Teachers on "The Novel of Slave Unrest." A student from Bennett College was responsible for her 2010 selection for the National Women's Hall of Fame.

www.ingramcontent.com/pod-product-compliance
Lightning Source LLC
LaVergne TN
LVHW041601070426
835507LV00011B/1226